ENGLISH TIME

WORKBOOK

4

Melanie Graham
Stanton Procter

OXFORD
UNIVERSITY PRESS

OXFORD
UNIVERSITY PRESS

198 Madison Avenue
New York, NY 10016 USA

Great Clarendon Street
Oxford OX2 6DP England

Oxford New York

Auckland Cape Town Dar es Salaam Hong Kong Karachi
Kuala Lumpur Madrid Melbourne Mexico City Nairobi
New Delhi Shanghai Taipei Toronto
With offices in
Argentina Austria Brazil Chile Czech Republic France Greece
Guatemala Hungary Italy Japan South Korea Poland Portugal
Singapore Switzerland Thailand Turkey Ukraine Vietnam

Oxford is a trademark of Oxford University Press.

ISBN-13: 978-0-19-436420-1
ISBN-10: 0-19-436420-8

Copyright © 2003 Oxford University Press

Editorial Manager: Nancy Leonhardt
Senior Editor: Lesley Koustaff
Editor: Paul Phillips
Associate Editors: Christine Hartzler, Sarah Wales McGrath
Senior Production Editor: Joseph McGasko
Production Editor: Arlette Lurie
Senior Designer: Maj-Britt Hagsted
Designer: Michael Steinhofer
Senior Art Buyer: Jodi Waxman
Art Buyer: Andrea Suffredini
Production Manager: Shanta Persaud
Production Coordinator: Zainaltu Jawat Ali

Illustrators: Mena Dolobowsky, Michelle Dorenkamp,
Kate Flanagan, Ann Iosa, Lynn Jeffery, Rita Lascaro, Susan Miller,
Vilma Ortiz-Dillon, Andrew Shiff

Original characters developed by Amy Wummer
Cover illustrations: Jim Talbot
Cover design: Silver Editions

Printing (last digit): 10 9 8

Printed in Hong Kong.

Do You Remember?

A. Read and match.

1. Excuse me. Can you help me? •
2. How much are these? •
3. I'm hungry. •
4. What's your address? •
5. Where's the trash can? •
6. What are you looking for? •

• Me, too. Let's have a snack.
• 23 Plain Road.
• Sure.
• My watch!
• They're one dollar each.
• It's over there. It's under the tree.

B. Read and write.

1.

Is this a wallet?
Yes, it is.

2.

Is that a river?
No, it isn't. It's   .

3.

Are these bean sprouts?

4.

Is that a puppy?

5.

Is he exercising?

6.

Was she at the bookstore?

C. Look, read, and write ✓ or X.

1.

He wants eggs.
He doesn't want pasta.

2.

How do they go to school?
They go to school by bicycle.

3.

Whose keys are these?
They're mine.

4.

Was she in the yard?
Yes, she was.

5.

It was at the restaurant.
It wasn't at the museum.

6.

When does he have a snack?
He has a snack in the afternoon.

7.

There are some trees.
There isn't any snow.

8.

Is there any hot sauce?
No, there isn't.

D. Look and write.

1.   2.   3.   4.   5.   6.

1. _____ab

2. _____esent

3. _____ile

4. _____ake

5. air_____ane

6. _____ead

A. Read and circle.

1. Wake up, / Watch TV, | Annie!

2. What | time / night | is it, Penny?

3. It's | three / seven | o'clock. It's time for | school. / breakfast.

4. Good. I'm | hungry. / happy.

5. Looks / Smells | good. What's for | breakfast? / homework?

6. We're having | bacon / bird | and | eggs. / ears.

7. Yum! | Their / My | favorite!

B. Read and match.

1. What's for breakfast?
   We're having cheese and bread.

2. What's for breakfast?
   We're having rice, fish, and fruit.

3. What's for breakfast?
   We're having cereal and juice.

A. Read and circle.

1.

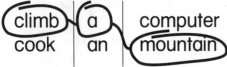

| (climb) | (a) | computer |
| cook | an | (mountain) |

2.

| listen | at | stories |
| laugh | to | sunrise |

3.

| climb | the | pans |
| clean | to | tent |

4.

| wash | the | sunrise |
| watch | your | pots |

5.

| play | cards |
| bake | jokes |

6.

| cook | bedroom |
| call | breakfast |

B. Look and write.

1.

I'm watching _____

_____.

2.

He isn't washing _____

_____.

3.

We're _____

_____.

4.

She's _____

_____.

Practice Time

A. Write the questions and answers.

1. you  ?

<u>Did you play cards?</u>
<u>No, I didn't. I</u>
_____ .

2. he  ?

_____
_____
_____

3. she  ?

_____
_____
_____

4. they  ?

_____
_____
_____

B. Read and write.

1. Did they cook breakfast?

_____

2. Did she laugh at jokes?

_____

3. _____

Yes, he did.

4. _____

Yes, they did.

A. Circle and write.

1.
ch
th
sh

____irt

2.
pr
br
dr

____esent

3.
sl
pr
pl

air____ane

4.
sm
sn
sp

____ile

5.
gr
tr
sh

____ee

6.
fl
cr
sl

____ower

7.
cr
dr
ch

____air

8.
th
br
tr

____ree

B. Read and write. Use some letters twice.

| tr | gr | pl | tch | th | sm | sp | fl | sh | cr | ch |

We like this park. There are ____owers and ____ees.
There is ____een ____ass. We ____y kites and ____ay
on the slide. We wa____ the fi____ in the ____eek
and catch ____iders. Our mo____ers ____ile and eat
pea____es and ____ums.

A. Unscramble and write. Then number the sentences in the correct order.

have / I / money. / Uh-oh! / don't / enough

_____ _____

so / really / It's / I'm / thirsty. / hot.

__1__ _____

a / Thanks / lot.

_____ _____

get / Let's / too. / Me, / juice. / some

_____ _____

do / kind / What / juice / of / want? / you

_____ _____

treat. / That's / It's / okay. / my

_____ _____

Here / are. / you

_____ _____

juice, / Orange / please.

_____ _____

B. Your turn. What do you want? Read and write.

I'm hungry. I want popcorn.

I'm _____ .

I want _____ .

A. Unscramble and write. Then number the words.

krind aosd opp

_____ _____

tae tocnot yndac

_____ _____

og on a dire

_____ _____

yub ckttsie

_____ _____

aket sciprute

_____ _____

niw a eripz

_____ _____

veah chunl

_____ _____

ees a hows

_____ _____

B. Look and write.

1. I have lunch at twelve o'clock.
2. I _____ .
3. _____
4. _____
5. _____
6. _____

Practice Time

A. Read and write.

1. drink ⟶ <u>drank</u>   2. eat ⟶ _____

3. win ⟶ _____   4. go ⟶ _____

5. see ⟶ _____   6. have ⟶ _____

7. buy ⟶ _____   8. take ⟶ _____

B. Look and write. Then number the pictures.

1. I _____ on a ride. I didn't _____ pictures.

2. I _____ tickets. I didn't _____ a prize.

3. I _____ pictures. I didn't _____ cotton candy.

C. Look and write.

1.

<u>She went on a ride.</u>
<u>She didn't _____</u>.

2.

<u>He _____</u>.
_____

3.

<u>They _____</u>.
_____

A. Which word has a different -ed sound? Read and circle.

1.
walked
played
asked

2.
baked
called
cleaned

3.
climbed
talked
chopped

4.
used
washed
danced

B. Read and write. Then write the words in the correct category.

1. brush   ⟶   __brushed__

2. water   ⟶   _____

3. kiss   ⟶   _____

4. watch   ⟶   _____

5. pull   ⟶   _____

6. play   ⟶   _____

7. laugh   ⟶   _____

8. listen   ⟶   _____

walked

used

C. Read the word. Then circle the words with the same -ed sound.

1. played

On Monday, Lisa watered the plants and brushed her hair.
Then she called a friend.

2. asked

On Saturday, Ted and Annie listened to music. They baked
cookies, too. Then they washed the pots and pans.

Conversation Time

A. Unscramble and write.

1.

 eLt em hlpe oyu, moM.

_____

 haTkns. eB farcelu. t'Is eahvy.

_____

2.

 oN emporbl. m'I rostgn.

_____

 eYs, ouy rae.

_____

3.

 pelH!

_____

 atWhc tou!

_____

4.

 rAe ouy koya?

_____

 I htkin os, ubt olok ta ym broasakted. _____

_____

B. Read and match.

1. Be back by six!

2. Be careful!

3. Sh! Be quiet!

A. Use the code to write the words. Then match.

m	n	o	p	q	r	s	t	u	v	w	x	y	z	a	b	c	d	e	f	g	h	i	j	k	l
↓	↓	↓	↓	↓	↓	↓	↓	↓	↓	↓	↓	↓	↓	↓	↓	↓	↓	↓	↓	↓	↓	↓	↓	↓	↓
a	b	c	d	e	f	g	h	i	j	k	l	m	n	o	p	q	r	s	t	u	v	w	x	y	z

1. <u>sweep</u> the <u>floor</u>
   eiqqb   rxaad

2. _____ the _____
   pa   xmgzpdk

3. _____ the _____
   tmzs gb   oxaftqe

4. _____ the _____
   ymwq   nqp

5. _____ the _____
   eqf   fmnxq

6. _____ the _____
   fmwq agf   smdnmsq

7. _____ the _____
   bgf mimk   sdaoqduqe

B. Read and write.

1.

What's she doing?

_____

_____

2.

What's he doing?

_____

_____

3.

What are they doing?

_____

_____

Practice Time

A. Read and match.

1. What did you do?
   I swept the floor.

2. What did you do?
   I hung up the clothes.

3. What did you do?
   We did the laundry.

B. Look, read, and write.

1. What did she do?

   _____

   _____

2. What did they do?

   _____

   _____

3. What _____?

   _____

   _____

4. _____

   _____

   _____

5. _____

   _____

   _____

6. _____

   _____

   _____

A. Read the word. Then circle the words with the same -ed sound.

1. | shouted | kissed   invited   weeded   played

2. | cooked | watched   waited   planned   counted

3. | greeted | chopped   dusted   planted   washed

B. Read and answer the questions.

Moe was busy on Saturday. In the morning, he played the piano and painted a picture. He called his friends, Sue and Jack, and invited them for lunch. Jack roasted some chicken. They ate under a tree. "Look at this," said Moe. "I planted a seed and now it's a tree!" In the afternoon, Moe, Sue, and Jack weeded the garden. Then they cleaned up.

1. Who did Moe invite for lunch?

_____

2. When did Moe paint a picture?

_____

3. Did Moe plant a weed?

_____

4. What did Moe, Sue, and Jack do in the afternoon?

_____

5. What did Jack roast?

_____

A. Match and write.

1. Are you okay? •   • I _____ so.

2. I don't have enough money. •   • We're _____ bacon and eggs.

3. I'm really thirsty. •   • _____. Be _____.

4. Let me help you. •   • Me, too. _____ get some _____.

5. What's for breakfast? •   • That's _____. It's my _____.

B. What did you do? Look and write.

| morning | afternoon | evening | night |

1. I fed the pets in the morning._____

2. I_____.

3. _____

4. _____

5. _____

6. _____

7. _____

8. _____

A. Read and write.

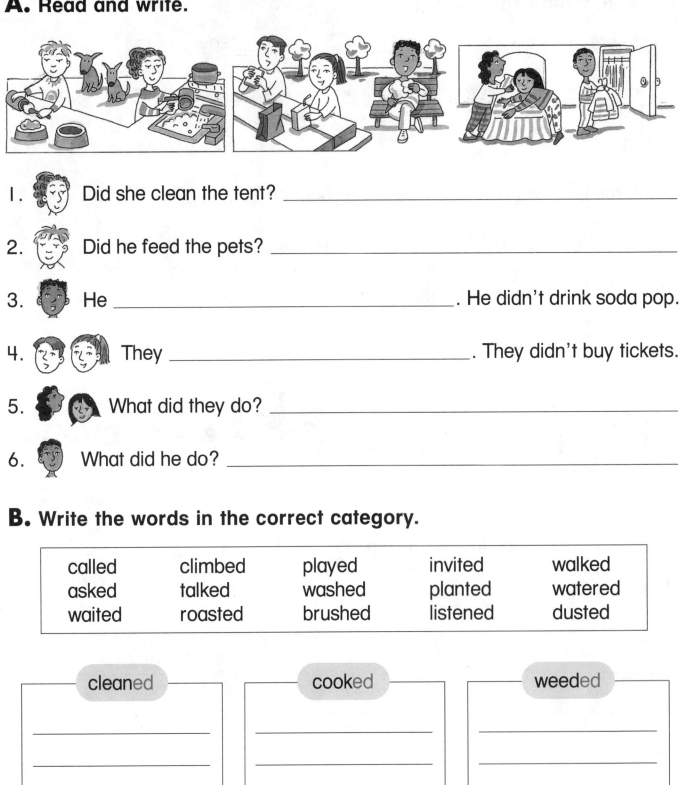

1. Did she clean the tent? _____

2. Did he feed the pets? _____

3. He _____. He didn't drink soda pop.

4. They _____. They didn't buy tickets.

5. What did they do? _____

6. What did he do? _____

B. Write the words in the correct category.

called	climbed	played	invited	walked
asked	talked	washed	planted	watered
waited	roasted	brushed	listened	dusted

cleaned

_____
_____
_____
_____
_____

cooked

_____
_____
_____
_____
_____

weeded

_____
_____
_____
_____
_____

A. **Fill in the blanks. Use some words twice.**

1. Excuse me. I'm _____ for the _____. Is it _____?

looking	Thank	really	you
You're	Walk	left	fun
museum	turn	right	far

2. Not _____.

3. _____ two blocks. Turn _____. It's on the right.

4. Did you say turn right or _____ _____?

5. Turn _____. It's on the _____.

6. _____ _____ very much.

7. _____ welcome. Have _____!

B. **Read and match.**

1. Walk two blocks. Turn left. It's on the left.

2. Walk one block. It's on the right.

3. Walk two blocks. Turn left. It's on the right.

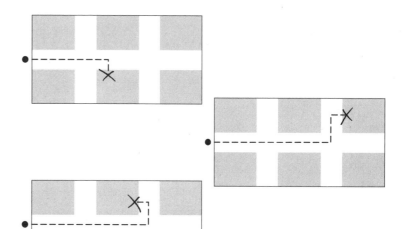

A. Unscramble and write.

teg a tuhcair	yub a tdoun	lami a telter
keat a xiat	isitv a ndrief	tren a diveo

1.

_____

2.

_____

3.

_____

4.

_____

5.

_____

6.

_____

B. What are they doing? Look and write.

1. They're **riding the bus.**   2. He's **getting** _____ .

3. She's _____ .   4. She's _____ .

5. They're _____ .   6. He's _____ .

16   Unit 4

A. Read. Then write ✓ and ✗.

1.

She's going to take a taxi.
She isn't going to ride the bus.

2.

They're going to see a movie.
They aren't going to rent a video.

3.

I'm going to mail a letter.
I'm not going to visit a friend.

4.

We're going to buy a donut.
We aren't going to get a haircut.

B. Look and write.

1.    She's _____ visit a friend.
_____ take a taxi.

 _____ take a taxi.
_____ visit a friend.

2.    _____
_____

 _____
_____

Phonics Time

A. Complete the puzzle.

Across

2. 5. 7.

Down

1.

3.

4.

6.

B. Read and circle the -le words.

Lana's uncle gave her a saddle. She rode her horse and
saw some cattle. She jumped in the lake and made a ripple.
She swam to the middle and saw a turtle.

"Little girl, give me an apple," said the turtle.

"I don't have an apple," said Lana, "but I have a saddle."

A. Read and circle.

What are you | eat? / ate? / eating?

Fried rice. | Try / Trying / Tried | some. It's good.

No, | thanks. / thank. / thanked.

Come / Came / Coming | on. Just a little.

Oh, all right. But not too much.

Here you | went. / going. / go.

Hey! | Its / It's / Is | delicious!

I | telling / told / tell | you so!

B. Read and match.

1. What is she drinking?
   Apple juice.

2. What are you eating?
   Popcorn.

3. What are you drinking?
   Soda pop.

4. What are they eating?
   Bacon and eggs.

A. Read and circle.

1.

a burrito
hot dogs

2.

a taco
tacos

3.

curry
iced tea

4. french fries
spaghetti

5.

lemonade
iced tea

6.

spaghetti
burritos

7.

a french fry
a hot dog

8.

lemonade
curry

B. Look and write.

1.

I want _____ .

I don't want _____ .

2.

_____

_____

3.

_____

_____

4.

_____

_____

C. Your turn. Read and write.

Do you want curry?

_____

_____

A. Read and match.

What are you going to have?   What are they going to have?

What's he going to have?   What's she going to have?

We're going to have some iced tea.   He's going to have a burrito.

They're going to have some curry.   She's going to have a taco.

B. Look and write.

1. What's _____ ?
   He's _____ .

2. _____

3. _____

4. _____

Phonics Time

A. Fill in the blanks.

paper	eraser	blister	ruler
marker	Peter	finger	computer

My name is _____ . I have a _____ on my _____ . I have a _____ on my desk. I have some _____ in my desk. I don't have an _____ , but I have a _____ and a _____ .

B. Fill in the blanks.

father

sister

lobster

peppers

butter

mother

cucumber

water

brother

dinner

It's time for _____ at my house. My _____ is going to have a hamburger. My _____ is going to have a _____ . My _____ is going to have _____ with _____ . My _____ is going to have roasted _____ . Digger is going to have some _____ .

A. Find the words. Then fill in the blanks and match.

(across)excusetimeyourfavoritemaththanksfunsubjectmusiclibraryclass

1. What's _____
   favorite _____?   •   •   Go straight. It's _____
                                                         from the _____ room.

2. _____ me. Where's   •   •   I like _____. It's
   the _____?   _____.

3. _____.   •   •   Great! That's my
                                                 _____.

4. Oh! It's _____ for
   art _____.   •   •   Sure.

B. Look at the chart. Write the questions and answers.

	Ted	Annie	Bob and Jan
Subject	English	math	English
Animal	lizard	dog	fish
Color	blue	red	green

1. <u>What's Annie's favorite animal? She likes dogs.</u>

2. _____ color? _____

3. _____ subject? _____

4. _____ animal? _____

Word Time

A. Look and match. Then write the phrases in the correct category.

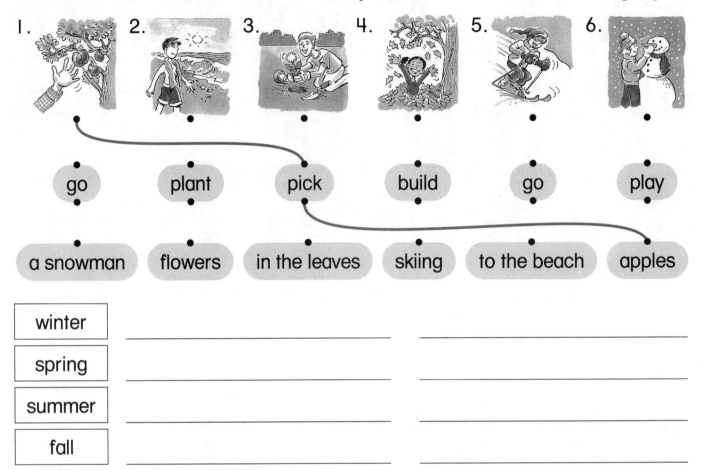

1. go
2. plant
3. pick
4. build
5. go
6. play

a snowman | flowers | in the leaves | skiing | to the beach | apples

winter	_____	_____
spring	_____	_____
summer	_____	_____
fall	_____	_____

B. Look and write.

1.

It's _____ . I'm going to go to the beach.

2.

It's _____ . I'm going to _____ .

3.

_____

_____

4.

_____

_____

A. Read and circle True or False.

1. He'll go skiing in the winter.
   He won't pick apples.   True   False

2. He'll go to the beach in the summer.
   He won't plant flowers.   True   False

3. She'll build a snowman in the fall.
   She won't pick apples.   True   False

4. She'll plant flowers in the spring.
   She won't play in the leaves.   True   False

B. Look and write.

1.

   He'll _____.
   He won't _____.

2.

   _____
   _____

3.

   _____
   _____

C. Your turn. What will you do?

I'll _____. I _____.

A. Circle and write.

1. al / au / aw

w____l

2. al / au / aw

dr_____

3. al / au / aw

s____cer

4. al / au / aw

ch____k

5. al / au / aw

t____k

6. al / au / aw

b____l

7. al / au / aw

cr____l

8. al / au / aw

w____k

B. Read and write.

1. Paul can't walk. Can he crawl?

_____

2. Does Paul draw on the wall with crayons?

_____

3. Who sees Paul draw?

_____

4. Does Paul like to draw on the wall?

_____

A. Read and write.

1.

Excuse me. Where's the library?
<u>Go straight. It's</u> _____

_____ .

2.

_____

_____

I like math. It's fun.

3.

What are you eating?
<u>Fried rice. Try</u> _____ .

_____

4.

_____

_____

I told you so.

B. Match and write.

1. see •   • a donut   _____

2. visit •   • a friend   _____

3. mail •   • a haircut   _____

4. build •   • a movie   <u>see a movie</u> _____

5. take •   • a taxi   _____

6. get •   • a snowman   _____

7. rent •   • a letter   _____

8. buy •   • a video   _____

Review 2

A. Look and write.

1.

He's going to _____ .

He isn't _____ .

2.

_____

_____

B. Look and write.

1.

What are you going to have? _____

_____

2.

_____

_____

C. Look and write.

1.

She'll plant flowers _____ .

She won't _____

_____ .

2.

_____

_____

D. Look and write.

1.    2.    3.    4.    5.    6.

lobst_____   tig_____   ch_____k   pudd_____   s_____cer   beet_____

A. Number the sentences in the correct order.

_____ Well, it's time to go.
Please make up your mind.

_____ Oh, I don't know. They're all cute.

_____ Great! Let's get it.

_____ Are you sure?

_____ Um, okay. I'll take this one.

_____ I'm positive!

_____ Dad, the cashier is over here.

_____ Which one do you want?

B. Look and match.

1.

2.

3.

4.

Which one do you want?

I'll take that one.

I don't know.

I'll take this one.

Word Time

A. Look. Then write the letter.

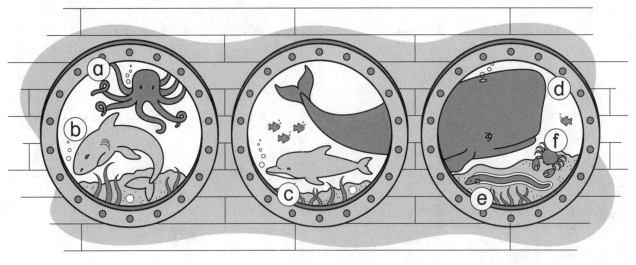

1. whale _____
2. eel _____
3. dolphin _____
4. octopus _____
5. shark _____
6. crab _____

B. Look and write.

1.

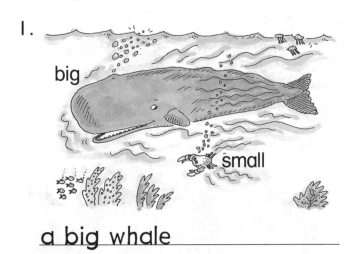

big

small

a big whale _____

a _____

2.

slow

fast

_____

_____

C. Your turn. Read and write.

Do you like sharks?   _____

Do you like dolphins?   _____

A. Read and write True or False.

1. The octopus is slower than the dolphin.   _____True_____
2. The dolphin is bigger than the shark.   _____
3. The eel is smaller than the whale.   _____
4. The whale is faster than the crab.   _____
5. The shark is slower than the octopus.   _____
6. The whale is bigger than the dolphin.   _____

B. Look and write.

1.	2.	3.	4.

1. (fast)   The _____ faster than _____.

2. (slow)   _____

3. (big)   _____

4. (small)   _____

A. Circle and write **ar** or **or**. Then number the pictures.

1.
| ar | or |
f____m

2.
| ar | or |
c____n

3.
| ar | or |
st____m

4.
| ar | or |
b____n

5.
| ar | or |
f____k

6.
| ar | or |
liz____d

B. Fill in the blanks.

dark	farm	horse	stories	barn	corn
cards	lizard	garden	yard	storm	popcorn

Today we visited Grandpa's _____. Grandpa grows peas and _____ in the _____. His _____ lives in a big, red _____. A small, green _____ lives there, too. We chased it across the _____.

There was a _____ in the evening. It rained and the sky was _____. We played _____ and listened to _____ in the house. Grandpa made _____.

A. Fill in the blanks.

car	cute	Quick	What	windows	is	going
what	worry	won't	monkey	scary	Look	not

1. Dad! Guess _____!

2. _____?

3. There's a _____ on the _____!

4. _____! Shut the _____!

5. _____! There it _____.

6. Oh, it's _____.

7. It's _____ cute. It's _____.

8. Don't _____. It _____ hurt you.

9. Aw! It's _____ away.

B. Look and write.

1. mouse / jump / bed

 Guess _____ ! _____

 There's _____ .

 Quick! Jump _____ .

2. lizard / shut / door

_____ _____

_____

 _____

Word Time

A. Unscramble, write, and circle.

1. aceehht
   _____

2. aeffgir
   _____

3. aceehimnpz
   _____

4. elrttu
   _____

5. aeehlnpt
   _____

6. aekns
   _____

B. Look and write.

1.

2.

3.

4.

She's _____ . _____ _____ _____

C. Look and write.

1.

The chimpanzee is short.

2.

_____

3.

_____

4.

_____

A. Circle and write.

1.

   Which one is the / tallest / shortest / (fattest)?
   The ___snake___ is the ___fattest___.

2.

   Which one is the / thinnest / tallest / shortest ?
   The _____ is the _____.

3.

   Which one is the / thinnest / shortest / fattest ?
   The _____ is the _____.

4.

   Which one is the / slowest / fattest / tallest ?
   The _____ is the _____.

B. Write the questions and answers.

1. tall

   Which one _____ ?
   The _____ .

2. short

   _____
   _____

3. fat

   _____
   _____

4. thin

   _____
   _____

A. Does it have ou or ow? Look and write.

1.

t___n

2.

c___

3.

m___se

4.

cl___d

5.

sh___t

6.

g___n

7.

h___se

8.

m___th

B. Fill in the blanks. Use some words twice.

shouting

mountain

flowers

house

mouth

cows

clouds

1. The mouse is climbing the _____ .

2. The man is _____ . His _____ is open.

3. There are five _____ .

4. The _____ are eating the grass.

5. There are two _____ in the sky.

6. There is a little _____ on the _____ .

Fill in the blanks.

| We won! | Yeah, it was. | We'll see. | And this time, we'll win. |
| I missed it! | It was close. | Congratulations. | Do you want to play again? |

1. Oh, no! _____

2. _____ We won!

3. _____

4. Nice game. _____

5. _____

6. _____

7. Sure. _____

8. _____

Word Time

A. Look and read. Then write.

Sunday	Monday	Tuesday	Wednesday	Thursday	Friday	Saturday
play Ping-Pong with Annie	go sailing with Ivy	in-line skate and listen to music with Matt	play badminton with Annie	go horseback riding with Joe	go fishing with Dad	snorkel with Matt and Kim

1. Ted will _____ with Matt and Kim on Saturday.

2. Ted will _____ with Annie on Sunday.

3. Ted will _____ with Joe _____.

4. Ted will _____ with Annie _____.

5. Ted will _____ on Friday.

6. Ted will _____ on Tuesday.

B. Look and write.

1.

He's going sailing. _____

2.

_____

3.

_____

4.

_____

5.

_____

6.

_____

Practice Time

A. Read and write the words. Then write ✓.

1. What do you like to do?

   I like to go horseback riding.

2. What does he like to do?

   _____ to go sailing.

3. What do you like to do?

   _____ to listen to music.

B. Look and write.

1. What does she like to do?

   _____

   _____

2. What does he like to do?

   _____

   _____

3. _____

   _____

   _____

4. _____

   _____

   _____

A. Which word has a different oo sound? Read and circle.

1.	2.	3.	4.	5.
noodle moon wood	book took moon	good rooster cookie	foot school wood	broom moon took

B. Read and match.

1. The baboon cooked some noodles. •

2. The poodle and the rooster looked at the moon. •

3. The moose stood on one foot. •

4. She sat on the wood and read a book. •

C. Look at B and write the oo words in the correct category.

cookie

_____ _____

_____ _____

_____ _____

broom

_____ _____

_____ _____

_____ _____

A. Look and write.

1.

Oh! _____

2.

Um, okay. I'll take that one.

3.

Dad, _____.

4.

Aw! _____

B. Read and write.

1.

Is it a giraffe?
No, it isn't.

It's a _____.

2.

Is it an eel?

_____

3.

Is it a chimpanzee?

_____

4.

Is it a shark?

_____

5.

Is it a crab?

_____

6.

Is it a dolphin?

_____

A. Read and write.

1. whale / big / elephant   <u>The whale is bigger than the elephant.</u>
2. cheetah / fast / turtle _____
3. eel / small / dolphin _____
4. crab / slow / giraffe _____

B. Look and write.

1. Which one is the _____? The giraffe _____.
2. _____ fattest? _____
3. Which one is the _____? The snake is the _____.
4. _____ shortest? _____

C. Write the words in the correct category.

| oo | <u>broom</u> _____ | ar | _____ | ou | _____ |

| oo | _____ | or | _____ | ow | _____ |

A. Fill in the blanks.

Wow! What a cool kite.

Thanks. _____ 1

_____ 2

No, it's true. I made it.

_____ 3

No, it was easy. _____ 4

Great. _____ 5

_____ 6 Let's get some.

You're kidding!	What do we need?
Paper and string.	Was it hard?
I made it myself.	I'll show you.

B. Read and match.

1. Was it easy?
   No, it was hard.

2. What a cool kite!
   Yeah. Sara made it.

3. What do we need?
   Tape, paper, and crayons.

A. Look. Then number the words.

_____ cycle   _____ read a comic book   _____ collect stickers   _____ sing

_____ paint   _____ take a nap   _____ make a video   _____ build a model

B. What will they do in the summer? Look and write.

1. _____
2. _____
3. _____
4. _____
5. _____
6. _____
7. _____
8. _____

1. He'll build a model. _____   2. She'll _____.

3. _____   4. _____

5. _____   6. _____

7. _____   8. _____

Practice Time

A. Read and write. Then number the pictures.

1. __I__ like cycling, but __I__ don't like collecting stickers.

2. _____ likes making videos, but _____ doesn't like building models.

3. _____ like painting, but _____ don't like taking naps.

4. _____ likes singing, but _____ doesn't like reading comic books.

B. Look and write.

1. She likes _____, but
she doesn't _____.

2. _____
_____

3. _____
_____

4. _____
_____

A. Does it have er, ir, or ur? Circle and write.

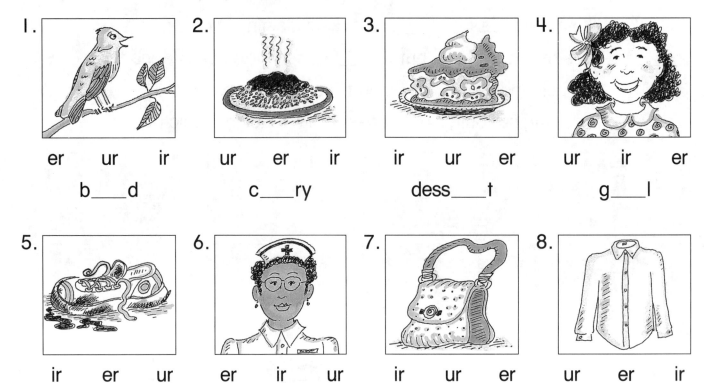

1. er   ur   ir
   b___d

2. ur   er   ir
   c___ry

3. ir   ur   er
   dess___t

4. ur   ir   er
   g___l

5. ir   er   ur
   d___ty

6. er   ir   ur
   n___se

7. ir   ur   er
   p___se

8. ur   er   ir
   sh___t

B. Fill in the blanks.

thirteen
shirt
dirty
thirsty
hurts
dessert
curry
bird
girl
purse

1. It can fly. It's small. It's a _____.

2. _____ is my favorite food. I eat it with rice.

3. Chocolate cake is my favorite _____.

4. Ted is a boy. Annie is a _____.

5. My keys and my wallet are in my _____.

6. The kitchen is _____. Let's clean up.

7. I want iced tea. I'm _____.

8. Ouch! My foot _____!

9. Ten and three is _____.

10. Gert bought jeans and a _____.

A. Fill in the blanks. Use some words twice.

Can	No	we	hurry	thirsty	buy	show
Yeah	a	planets	the	snack	We	great
Wow	I'm	catch	stars	bus	gift	time

1. _____! Did you see all the _____ and _____?

2. _____! That was a _____.

3. Ms. Apple, can we go to the _____ bar?

4. _____ we go to the _____ shop?

5. _____, kids. _____ don't have _____.

6. Aw. But I want to _____ for my dad.

7. And _____.

8. Please, Ms. Apple. We'll _____.

9. Sorry, kids. _____ have to _____.

B. Look and write.

bookstore / buy a book

 Can _____

_____?

 No, Ted. We _____

_____.

 Aw. _____

_____

Word Time

A. Which planet is it? Read and write.

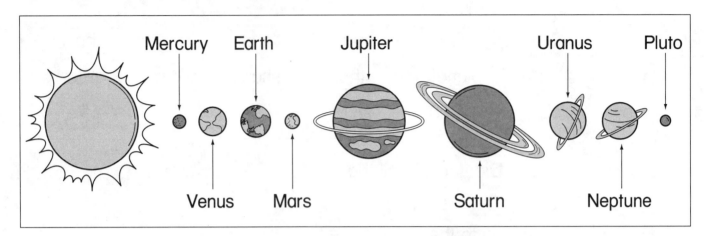

1. It's next to Mercury. It's smaller than Earth. <u>It's Venus.</u>
2. It's next to Saturn, but it isn't Jupiter. <u>It's   .</u>
3. It's next to the smallest planet. It's smaller than Jupiter. _____
4. It's the smallest planet. _____
5. It's next to Venus. It's smaller than Venus. _____
6. It's next to Mars, but it isn't next to Venus. _____
7. It's our planet. We live here. _____
8. It's next to Jupiter, but it isn't next to Uranus. _____
9. It isn't next to Pluto, but it's next to Uranus. _____

B. Write the names of the planets.

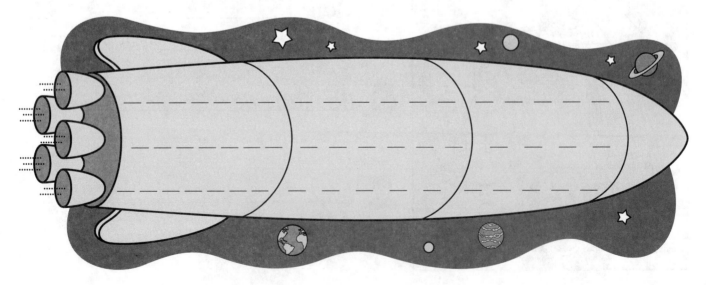

A. Number the sentences.

1.

2.

3.

4.

_____ She wants to see Pluto.
Let her look.

_____ He wants to see Saturn.
Let him look.

_____ I want to see Neptune.
Let me look.

_____ They want to see Venus.
Let them look.

B. Read and write.

1. she → <u>her</u>   2. I → _____   3. we → _____   4. they → _____   5. he → _____

C. Read and write.

1. He / Mercury

<u>He wants to see Mercury. Let him look.</u>

2. I / Pluto

_____

3. They / Jupiter

_____

4. We / Mars

_____

5. She / Venus

_____

A. Does it have oi or oy? Write and match.

1. R___ is a b___. J___ce is a girl. •

2. R___ p___nted at the ___sters
   in the f___l.

3. R___ b___led some ___sters. •

4. J___ce br___led some ___sters. •

5. J___ce wanted s___ sauce and
   R___ wanted ___l.

6. They ate the ___sters and jumped
   for j___.

B. Follow the oy words.

12

A. Fill in the blanks. Then number the sentences.

together dance practice have dancing do dancer idea That's enough well

1 You _____ really well.

Sure you _____. ___
You're a good _____.

___ But I don't practice _____.

Well, _____ makes perfect. ___

___ _____ a great idea. Thanks.

Thanks. I love _____. ___

___ I don't dance very _____.

I _____ an _____. ___
Let's practice _____.

B. Look and write.

You paint _____.

Thanks. I _____.

I don't _____.

Sure _____. You're a _____.

Word Time

A. Read and match.

1. musician
2. nurse
3. computer programmer
4. engineer
5. artist

B. Read and write.

Monday

Today is Sunday. What are they going to do on Monday?

1. She's a musician. <u>She's going to</u> _____.

2. He's a vet. _____

3. They're engineers. _____

4. She's a computer programmer. _____

5. They're artists. _____

6. He's a nurse. _____

A. Read and write.

1. Why does she want to be _____?
   Because she likes _____.

2. Why does he want to be _____?
   _____

3. Why do they want to be _____?
   _____

4. Why does he want to be _____?
   _____

5. Why does she want to be _____?
   _____

6. Why does she want to be _____?
   _____

B. Your turn. Read and write.

Why do you want to be a _____?

Because _____
_____.

A. Read and write. Use some letters twice.

ar	au	er	or	ow	ou	oi	ur	ir	oo

1.

P_____l and Patty went shopping.
P_____l bought a sh_____t. Patty
bought a p_____se. The cl_____k was
very happy!

2.

Walt c_____ked lunch today. He
b_____led some instant n_____dles.
"Yum!" said Sue. But there was a
c_____n in the n_____dles and a
mark_____ in the salad!

3.

Carl went to the p_____k. He ate
d_____t with a f_____k and got very
d_____ty. He saw a d_____k cl_____d
and thought, "I can take a sh_____er in
the rain!"

B. Do they both have the same vowel sound? Look and write ✓ or ✗.

1.
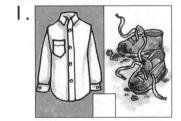

2.
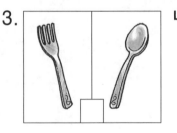

3.

4.

A. Read and match. Then fill in the blanks.

dancer	easy	dancing	great	idea	myself

1. Was it hard? •

   • Sure you do. You're a good

   _____.

2. I don't dance very well. •

   • That's a great _____.
   Thanks.

3. Did you see all the planets and stars? •

   • Thanks. I love _____.

4. I have an idea. Let's practice together. •

   • No, it was _____.

5. Wow! What a cool kite! •

   • Yeah! That was a _____
   show.

6. You dance really well. •

   • Thanks. I made it _____.

B. Circle the odd word.

1. | collect stickers | artist | paint | cycle |

2. | build things | Mars | Mercury | Jupiter |

3. | read comic books | build models | computer programmer | make videos |

4. | Venus | vet | Earth | Pluto |

5. | engineer | help animals | take care of people | take a nap |

6. | sing | cycle | paint | nurse |

A. Read. Then answer the questions.

Hi. My name is Burt. This is Matt and this is Nell. Matt is twelve years old. Nell is eleven. Matt likes building things. He wants to be an engineer. Matt likes playing the violin, but he doesn't like singing. Nell likes singing, but she doesn't like playing the violin. She wants to be an artist. She likes drawing.

1. Does Matt like singing?

_____

2. Why does Nell want to be an artist?

_____

3. Does Nell like playing the violin?

_____

4. Why does Matt want to be an engineer?

_____

B. Look and write.

1.

_____ster

2.

dess_____t

3.

b_____d

4.

p_____se

5.

sp_____n

6.

cl_____d

7.

p_____nt

8.
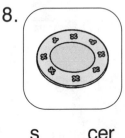

s_____cer

A. Read and match.

1. What are you eating? •

2. Let me help you. •

3. What time is it? •

4. Where's the music room? •

5. What kind of juice do you want? •

6. I'm looking for the museum. Is it far? •

• Pineapple juice, please.

• Not really.

• It's across from the library.

• Thanks. Be careful.

• Fried rice.

• Seven o'clock. It's time for breakfast.

B. Read and match.

1. Can we go to the snack bar? •

2. Wow! What a cool kite! •

3. Are you sure? •

4. It's not cute. It's scary. •

5. You dance really well. •

6. We won! We won! •

• I'm positive.

• Thanks. I love dancing.

• Don't worry. It won't hurt you.

• Congratulations!

• Thanks. I made it myself.

• No, we don't have time.

Find 14 activities. Then write the words.

1. <u>ride a horse</u>
2. _____

3. _____
4. _____

5. _____
6. _____

7. _____
8. _____

9. _____
10. _____

11. _____
12. _____

13. _____
14. _____

A. Match and write.

1. What are you going to have? •   • Yes, _____.

2. She drank soda pop. •   • I'm _____ tacos.

3. What did she do? •   • _____ not going to see a movie.

4. He'll play in the leaves in the fall. •   • She _____ win a prize.

5. Did they watch the sunrise? •   • _____ won't _____ the beach.

6. I'm going to rent a video. •   • She swept _____.

B. Write and match.

1. Why _____ to be an artist? •   • bigger than the dolphin.

2. _____ he like to do? •   • Let her look.

3. Which one is the _____? •   • but I don't like cycling.

4. She _____ Mars. •   • Because I like drawing.

5. _____ like painting, •   • He likes to go sailing.

6. _____ whale _____ •   • The giraffe is the tallest.

A. **What vowel sound does it have? Look and match.**

1.   2.   3.   4.

aw •   ar •   ur •   er •   ou •   oo •   oi •   or •

5.   6.   7.   8.

B. **Which word has a different -ed sound? Read and circle.**

1.
walked
kissed
weeded
chopped

2.
planted
cleaned
invited
dusted

3.
called
played
baked
stayed

4.
waited
dusted
roasted
washed

C. Read.

Mark likes to look at the moon. His friends Paul and Roy like to look at it, too. On Monday, Mark invited Paul and Roy for dinner. They cooked noodles and made apple pie for dessert. Then they cleaned up. Mark said, "Let's hurry! It's time to look at the moon!" They climbed the mountain by the town and looked at the moon and stars. It was a good night, and Mark was happy.

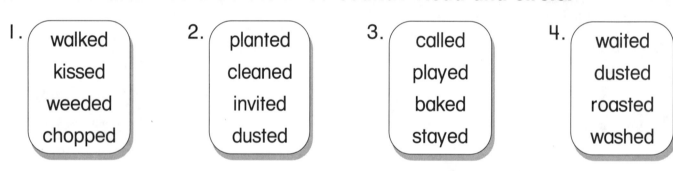